NG ALONG WITH

GW00362139

WISE PUBLICATIONS
PART OF THE MUSIC SALES GROUP

LONDON / NEW YORK / PARIS / SYDNEY / COPENHAGEN / BERLIN / MADRID / HONG KONG / TOKYO

Published by
Wise Publications
14-15 Berners Street,
London W1T 3LJ, UK.

Exclusive Distributors:
Music Sales Limited
Distribution Centre, Newmarket Road,
Bury St Edmunds, Suffolk IP33 3YB, UK.
Music Sales Corporation
180 Madison Avenue, 24th Floor,
New York NY 10016, USA.
Music Sales Pty Limited
Units 3-4, 17 Willfox Street, Condell Park
NSW 2200, Australia.

Order No. AM1007061
ISBN 978-1-78305-204-2

Your Guarantee of Quality
As publishers, we strive to produce every book to the
highest commercial standards.
This book has been carefully designed to minimise awkward
page turns and to make playing from it a real pleasure.
Particular care has been given to specifying acid-free, neutral-sized paper
made from pulps which have not been elemental chlorine bleached.
This pulp is from farmed sustainable forests and was
produced with special regard for the environment.
Throughout, the printing and binding have been planned to
ensure a sturdy, attractive publication which should give years of enjoyment.
If your copy fails to meet our high standards,
please inform us and we will gladly replace it.

www.musicsales.com

PART ONE

ADELE

CHASING PAVEMENTS

I've made up my mind,
Don't need to think it over.
If I'm wrong I am right,
Don't need to look no further.
This ain't lust, I know this is love.
But if I tell the world, I'll never say enough,
'Cause it was not said to you,
And that's exactly what I need to do
If I end up with you.

Should I give up?
Or should I just keep chasing pavements
Even if it leads nowhere?
Or would it be a waste even if I knew my place?
Should I leave it there?
Should I give up?
Or should I just keep chasing pavements
Even if it leads nowhere?

I build myself up and fly around in circles,
Waiting as my heart drops
And my back begins to tingle.
Finally, could this be it or:

Should I give up?
Or should I just keep chasing pavements
Even if it leads nowhere?
Or would it be a waste even if I knew my place?
Should I leave it there?
Should I give up?
Or should I just keep chasing pavements
Even if it leads nowhere?
Yeah.

Should I give up?
Or should I just keep chasing pavements
Even if it leads nowhere?
Or would it be a waste even if I knew my place?
Should I leave it there?
Should I give up?
Or should I just keep on chasing pavements?
Should I just keep on chasing pavements?

Or should I give up?
Or should I just keep chasing pavements
Even if it leads nowhere?
Or would it be a waste even if I knew my place?
Should I leave it there?
Should I give up?
Or should I just keep chasing pavements
Even if it leads nowhere?

HOMETOWN GLORY

I've been walking in the same way as I did;
Missing out the cracks in the pavement
And tutting my heel and strutting my feet.
"Is there anything I can do for you, dear?
Is there anyone I could call?"
"No and thank you, please Madam.
I ain't lost just wandering."

Round my hometown memories are fresh.
Round my hometown, oh, the people I've met
Are the wonders of my world,
Are the wonders of my world,
Are the wonders of this world,
Are the wonders of now.

I like it in the city
When the air is so thick and opaque.
I love to see everybody in short skirts,
Shorts and shades.
I like it in the city when two worlds collide;
You get the people and the government,
Everybody taking different sides.

Shows that we ain't gonna stand it.
Shows that we are united.
Shows that we ain't gonna take it.
Shows that we ain't gonna stand it.
Shows that we are united.

Round my hometown memories are fresh.
Round my hometown, oh, the people I've met.

(Vocal ad lib.)

Doot 'n' doot 'n' doot 'n' doo oh.
Yeah, yeah.

Are the wonders of my world,
Are the wonders of my world,
Are the wonders of this world,
Are the wonders of my world,
Of my world, yeah.
Of my world, of my world, yeah.

MAKE YOU FEEL MY LOVE

When the rain is blowing in your face,
And the whole world is on your case,
I could offer you a warm embrace
To make you feel my love.

When the evening shadows and the stars appear,
And there is no one there to dry your tears,
I could hold you for a million years
To make you feel my love.

I know you haven't made your mind up yet,
But I could never do you wrong.
I've known it from the moment that we met;
No doubt in my mind where you belong.

I'd go hungry I'd go black and blue,
I'd go crawling down the avenue.
Know there's nothing that I wouldn't do
To make you feel my love.

The storms are raging on the rolling sea,
And on the highway of regret
The winds of change are blowing wild and free,
You ain't seen nothing like me yet.

I could make you happy,
Make your dreams come true,
Nothing that I wouldn't do,
Go to the ends of the earth for you
To make you feel my love,
To make you feel my love.

ROLLING IN THE DEEP

There's a fire starting in my heart,
Reaching a fever pitch
And it's bringing me out the dark.
Finally I can see you crystal clear.
Go ahead and sell me out
And I'll lay your s**t bare.
See how I'll leave with every piece of you.
Don't underestimate the things that I will do.
There's a fire starting in my heart,
Reaching a fever pitch
And it's bringing me out the dark.
The scars of your love remind me of us.
They keep me thinking that we almost had it all.
The scars of your love, they leave me breathless.
I can't help feeling:

We could have had it all.
Rolling in the deep.
You had my heart and soul 'side of your hand.
And you played it to the beat.

Baby, I have no story to be told.
But I've heard one on you
Now I'm gonna make your head burn.
Think of me in the depths of your despair.
Make a home down there
As mine sure won't be shared.
The scars of your love remind me of us.
They keep me thinking that we almost had it all.
The scars of your love, they leave me breathless.
I can't help feeling:

We could have had it all.
Rolling in the deep.
You had my heart and soul 'side of your hand.
And you played it to the beat.
Could have had it all.
Rolling in the deep.
You had my heart and soul 'side of your hand.
But you played it with a beating.

Throw your soul through every open door.
Count your blessings to find what you look for.
Turn my sorrows into treasured gold.
You'll pay me back in kind
And reap just what you've sown.

We could have had it all.
We could have had it all.
It all. It all. It all.

We could have had it all.
Rolling in the deep.
You had my heart and soul 'side of your hand.
And you played it to the beat.
Could have had it all.
Rolling in the deep.
You had my heart and soul 'side of your hand.
And you played it, you played it, you played it,
You played it to the beat.

SET FIRE TO THE RAIN

I let it fall, my heart.
And as it fell you rose to claim it.
It was dark and I was over
Until you kissed my lips and you saved me.
My hands they were strong,
But my knees were far too weak
To stand in your arms
Without falling to your feet.

But there's a side to you that I never knew,
Never knew.
All the things you'd say, they were never true,
Never true.
And the games you'd play you would always win,
Always win.

But I set fire to the rain.
Watched it pour as I touched your face.
When it burned, well, I cried
'Cause I heard it screaming out your name.
Your name.

When I lay with you I could stay there,
Just close my eyes,
Feel you here forever.
You and me together, nothing gets better.
'Cause there's a side to you that I never knew,
Never knew.
All the things you'd say, they were never true,
Never true.
And the games you'd play you would always win,
Always win.

But I set fire to the rain.
Watched it pour as I touched your face.
When it burned, well, I cried
'Cause I heard it screaming out your name.
Your name.

I set fire to the rain.
And I threw us into the flames.
When we fell, something died
'Cause I knew that that was the last time,
The last time.

Sometimes I wake up by the door
That heart you caught must be waiting for ya.
Even now when we're already over.
I can't help myself from looking for you.

I set fire to the rain.
Watched it pour as I touched your face.
When it burned, well, I cried
'Cause I heard it screaming out your name.
Your name.

I set fire to the rain.
And I threw us into the flames.
When we fell, something died
'Cause I knew that that was the last time,
The last time.

(Vocal ad lib. to end)

SOMEONE LIKE YOU

I heard that you're settled down.
That you found a girl and you're married now.
I heard that your dreams came true.
Guess she gave you things I didn't give to you.
Old friend, why are you so shy?
Ain't like you to hold back, or hide from the light.

I hate to turn up out of the blue uninvited
But I couldn't stay away.
I couldn't fight it.
I had hoped you'd see my face
And that you'd be reminded
That for me it isn't over.

Never mind I'll find someone like you.
I wish nothing but the best for you two.
Don't forget me, I beg.
I'll remember you said
Sometimes it lasts and loves
But sometimes it hurts instead.
Sometimes it lasts and loves
But sometimes it hurts instead.

You know how the time flies,
Only yesterday was the time of our lives.
We were born and raised in a summer haze.
Bound by the surprise of our glory days.

I hate to turn up out of the blue uninvited
But I couldn't stay away.
I couldn't fight it.
I had hoped you'd see my face
And that you'd be reminded
That for me it isn't over.

Never mind I'll find someone like you.
I wish nothing but the best for you two.
Don't forget me, I beg.
I'll remember you said
Sometimes it lasts and loves
But sometimes it hurts instead.

Nothing compares, no worries or cares,
Regrets and mistakes, they are memories made.
Who would have known how bittersweet
This would taste?

Never mind I'll find someone like you.
I wish nothing but the best for you.
Don't forget me, I beg.
I'll remember you said
Sometimes it lasts and loves
But sometimes it hurts instead.

Never mind I'll find someone like you.
I wish nothing but the best for you two.
Don't forget me, I beg.
I'll remember you said
Sometimes it lasts and loves
But sometimes it hurts instead.
Sometimes it lasts and loves
But sometimes it hurts instead.

CHASING PAVEMENTS

WORDS & MUSIC BY ADELE ADKINS & EG WHITE

1. I've made up my mind,_ don' need to think it o-ver. If I'm wrong I am_ right,_ don't need to look no fur-ther. This ain' lust, I_____ know this is love. 2. But if

HOMETOWN GLORY

WORDS & MUSIC BY ADELE ADKINS

15

MAKE YOU FEEL MY LOVE

WORDS & MUSIC BY BOB DYLAN

23

24

to make you feel my love.

ROLLING IN THE DEEP

WORDS & MUSIC BY ADELE ADKINS & PAUL EPWORTH

1.There's a_____ fire_____ start-ing in my_____ heart,

2. See how___ I'll___ leave with ev-'ry piece of you.

reach-ing___ a fe-ver pitch and it's bring-ing me out the dark.___

Don't un-der-es-ti-mate the things that I will do.___

29

31

33

SET FIRE TO THE RAIN

WORDS & MUSIC BY FRASER SMITH & ADELE ADKINS

1. I let it fall, my heart. And as it fell you rose to claim it. It was dark and I was o-ver until you kissed my lips and you saved me. My

41

SOMEONE LIKE YOU

WORDS & MUSIC BY ADELE ADKINS & DANIEL WILSON

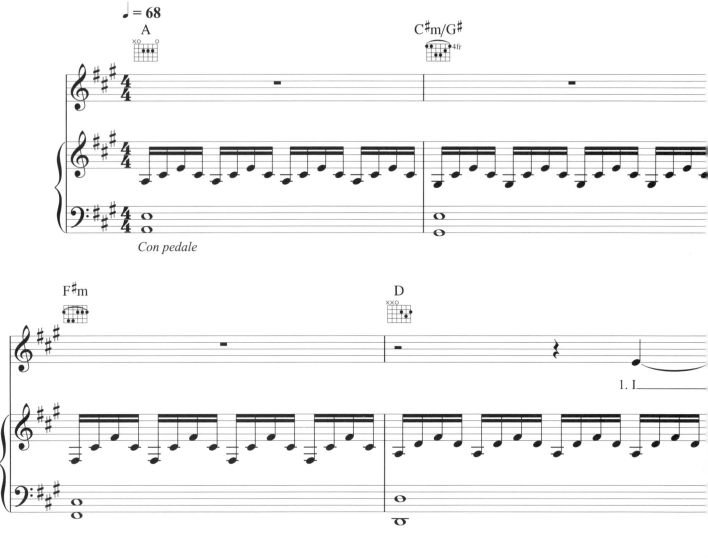

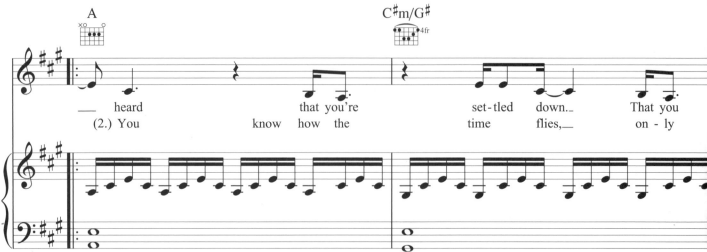

43

you to hold back, or hide from the light.

hate to turn up out of the blue un-in-vit-ed but I could-n't stay a - way. I could-n't fight it. I h

hoped you'd see my face and that you'd be re-mind-ed that for me it is-n't o - ver.

1° only

2° only

44

PART TWO

LILY ALLEN

22

When she was twenty-two
The future looked bright
But she's nearly thirty now
And she's out every night
I see that look in her face
She's got that look in her eye
She's thinking how did I get here
And wondering why

It's sad, but it's true, how society says
Her life is already over
There's nothing to do
And there's nothing to say
Until the man of her dreams
Comes along, picks her up
And puts her over his shoulder
It seems so unlikely in this day and age

She's got an alright job
But it's not a career
Whenever she thinks about it
It brings her to tears
'Cause all she wants is a boyfriend
She gets one-night stands
She's thinking how did I get here
I'm doing all that I can

It's sad, but it's true, how society says
Her life is already over
There's nothing to do
And there's nothing to say
Until the man of her dreams
Comes along, picks her up
And puts her over his shoulder
It seems so unlikely in this day and age

It's sad, but it's true, how society says
Her life is already over
There's nothing to do
And there's nothing to say
Until the man of her dreams
Comes along, picks her up
And puts her over his shoulder
It seems so unlikely in this day and age

THE FEAR

I wanna be rich
And I want lots of money
I don't care about clever
I don't care about funny
I want loads of clothes
And f**kloads of diamonds
I heard people die
While they're trying to find them

And I'll take my clothes off
And it will be shameless
'Cause everyone knows
It's how you get famous
I'll look at the Sun
And I'll look in the Mirror
I'm on the right track
Yeah, I'm onto a winner

And I don't know what's right
And what's real anymore
And I don't know how
I'm meant to feel anymore
When do you think
It will all become clear?
'Cause I'm being taken
Over by the fear

Life's about film stars
And less about mothers
It's all about fast cars
And cussin' each other
But it doesn't matter
'Cause I'm packing plastic
And that's what makes my life
So f**king fantastic

And I am a weapon
Of massive consumption
And it's not my fault
It's how I'm programmed to function
I'll look at the Sun
And I'll look in the Mirror
I'm on the right track
Yeah, we're onto a winner

And I don't know what's right
And what's real anymore
And I don't know
How I'm meant to feel anymore
When do you think
It will all become clear?
'Cause I'm being taken
Over by the fear

Forget about guns
And forget ammunition
'Cause I'm killing them all
On my own little mission
Now, I'm not a saint
But I'm not a sinner
And everything's cool
As long as I'm getting thinner

And I don't know what's right
And what's real anymore
And I don't know how
I'm meant to feel anymore
When do you think
It will all become clear?
'Cause I'm being taken
Over by the fear

LDN

Riding through the city on my bike all day
'Cause the filth took away my licence
It doesn't get me down and I feel okay
'Cause the sights that I'm seeing are priceless

Everything seems to look as it should
But I wonder what goes on behind doors
A fellow looking dapper and he's sitting with a slapper
Then I see it's a pimp and his crack whore

You might laugh, you might frown
Walking round London town

Sun is in the sky; oh why, oh why
Would I wanna be anywhere else?
Sun is in the sky; oh why, oh why
Would I wanna be anywhere else?

When you look with your eyes
Everything seems nice
But, if you look twice
You can see it's all lies

There was a little old lady who was
Walking down the road
She was struggling with bags from Tesco
There were people from the city
Having lunch in the park
I believe that it's called al fresco

When a kid came along to offer a hand
But, before she had time to accept it
Hits her over the head, doesn't care if she's dead
'Cause he's got all her jewellery and wallet

You might laugh, you might frown
Walking round London town

Sun is in the sky; oh why, oh why
Would I wanna be anywhere else?
Sun is in the sky; oh why, oh why
Would I wanna be anywhere else?

When you look with your eyes
Everything seems nice
But, if you look twice
You can see it's all lies

Life: yeah, that's city life
Yeah, that's city life
Yeah, that's city life

Life: yeah, that's city life
Yeah, that's city life
Yeah, that's city life

Sun is in the sky; oh why, oh why
Would I wanna be anywhere else?
Sun is in the sky; oh why, oh why
Would I wanna be anywhere else?

Sun is in the sky; oh why, oh why
Would I wanna be anywhere else?
Sun is in the sky; oh why, oh why
Would I wanna be anywhere else?

When you look with your eyes
Everything seems nice
But, if you look twice
You can see it's all lies

When you look with your eyes
Everything seems nice
But, if you look twice
You can see it's all lies

NOT FAIR

Oh, he treats me with respect
He says he loves me all the time
He calls me fifteen times a day
He likes to make sure that I'm fine
You know I've never met a man
Who's made me feel quite so secure
He's not like all them other boys
They're all so dumb and immature

There's just one thing
That's getting in the way
When we go up to bed
You're just no good
It's such a shame
I look into your eyes
I want to get to know you
And then you make this noise
And it's apparent it's all over

It's not fair and
I think you're really mean
I think you're really mean
I think you're really mean
Oh, you're supposed to care
But you never make me scream
You never make me scream

Oh, it's not fair and it's really not okay
It's really not okay, it's really not okay
Oh, you're supposed to care
But all you do is take
Yeah, all you do is take

Oh, I lie here in the wet patch
In the middle of the bed
I'm feeling pretty damn hard done by
I spent ages giving head
Then I remember all the nice things
That you've ever said to me
Maybe I'm just overreacting
Maybe you're the one for me

There's just one thing
That's getting in the way
When we go up to bed
You're just no good
It's such a shame
I look into your eyes
I want to get to know you
And then you make this noise
And it's apparent it's all over

Chorus

There's just one thing
That's getting in the way
When we go up to bed
You're just no good
It's such a shame
I look into your eyes
I want to get to know you
And then you make this noise
And it's apparent it's all over

It's not fair and
I think you're really mean
I think you're really mean
I think you're really mean
Oh, you're supposed to care
But you never make me scream
You never make me scream

Oh, it's not fair and it's really not okay
It's really not okay, it's really not okay
Oh, you're supposed to care
But all you do is take
Yeah, all you do is take

OH MY GOD

Time on your side that will never end
The most beautiful thing you can ever spend
But you work in a shirt with your name tag on it
Drifting apart like a plate tectonic
It don't matter to me
'Cause all I wanted to be
Was a million miles from here
Somewhere more familiar

Too much time spent dragging the past up
I didn't see you not looking when I messed up
Settling down in your early twenties
Sucked more blood than a back street dentist
It don't matter to me
'Cause all I wanted to be
Was a million miles from here
Somewhere more familiar

And oh my god I can't believe it
I've never been this far away from home
And oh my god I can't believe it
I've never been this far away from home
And oh my god I can't believe it
I've never been this far away from home
And oh my god I can't believe it
I've never been this far away from home

Great rulers make for a greater glory
The only thing growing is our history
Knock me down I'll get right back up again
I come back stronger than a powered up Pacman
It don't matter to me
'Cause all I wanted to be
Was a million miles from here
Somewhere more familiar

And oh my god I can't believe it
I've never been this far away from home
And oh my god I can't believe it
I've never been this far away from home
And oh my god I can't believe it
I've never been this far away from home
And oh my god I can't believe it
I've never been this far away from home

Vocal/Instrumental ad lib.

And oh my god I can't believe it
I've never been this far away from home
And oh my god I can't believe it
I've never been this far away from home
And oh my god I can't believe it
I've never been this far away from home
And oh my god I can't believe it
I've never been this far away from...

SMILE

When you first left me
I was wanting more
But you were f**king that girl next door
What'd you do that for?

When you first left me
I didn't know what to say
I'd never been on my own that way
Just sat by myself all day

I was so lost back then
But, with a little help from my friends
I found the light in the tunnel at the end

Now you're calling me up on the phone
So you can have a little whine and a moan
It's only because you're feeling alone

At first, when I see you cry
It makes me smile, yeah, it makes me smile
At worst, I feel bad for a while
But then I just smile; I go ahead and smile

Whenever you see me
You say that you want me back
And I tell you it don't mean jack
No, it don't mean jack

I couldn't stop laughing
No, I just couldn't help myself
See, you messed up my mental health
I was quite unwell

I was so lost back then
But, with a little help from my friends
I found the light in the tunnel at the end

Now you're calling me up on the phone
So you can have a little whine and a moan
It's only because you're feeling alone

At first, when I see you cry
It makes me smile, yeah, it makes me smile
At worst, I feel bad for a while
But then I just smile; I go ahead and smile

La la la la la la la la la la la la la la la la la la la la
La la la la la la la la la la la la la la la la la la la la la

At first, when I see you cry
It makes me smile, yeah, it makes me smile
At worst, I feel bad for a while
But then I just smile; I go ahead and smile

At first, when I see you cry
It makes me smile, yeah, it makes me smile
At worst, I feel bad for a while
But then I just smile; I go ahead and smile

22

WORDS & MUSIC BY LILY ALLEN & GREG KURSTIN

7

-ver.___ There's noth-ing to do___ and there's noth-ing to

___ say._____ Un-til the man of her dreams

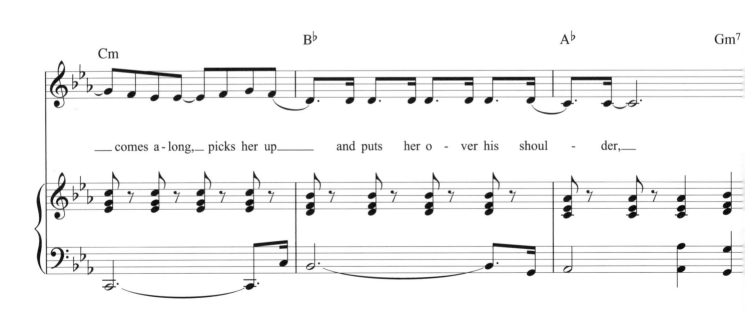

___ comes a-long,___ picks her up___ and puts her o-ver his shoul - der,___

it seems so un - like - ly   in this day and____ age._____

It's sad, but it's true,__

THE FEAR

WORDS & MUSIC BY LILY ALLEN & GREG KURSTIN

1. I wan-na be rich and I want lots of mo-
2. Life's a-bout film stars and less a-bout mot-

-ey, I don't care a-bout clev-er, I don't care a-bout fun-ny. I want loads of cloth-
-ers, it's all a-bout fast cars and cus-sin' each oth-er. But it does-n't mat-

13

clear?   'Cause I'm___ be - ing ta -

_- ken o - ver by the___ fear.___

but I'm not a sin - ner, and ev - 'ry - thing's cool___ as long as I'm get - ting thin -

- ner. And I don't know___

LDN

WORDS & MUSIC BY IYIOLA BABALOLA, DARREN LEWIS, LILY ALLEN
& ARTHUR 'DUKE' REID

life._____ Yeah, that's_ ci - ty life._____

Sun is in the sky; oh why, oh why would I

wan - na be an - y - where else?_____ Sun is in the sky; oh

why, oh why would I wan - na be an - y - where else?_____

NOT FAIR

WORDS & MUSIC BY LILY ALLEN & GREG KURSTIN

fif - teen times a day,____ he likes to make sure that I'm fine.____ You know I've
pret - ty_ damn hard done____ by, I spent ag - es giv - ing head.____ Then I re -

nev - er met a man____ who's made me feel quite so se - cure,____ he's not like
-mem - ber all_ the nice____ things that you've ev - er said to me,____ may - be I'm

all them oth - er boys____ they're all so dumb and im - ma - ture.____ } There's just one
just o - ver - re - act - ing, may - be you're the one_ for me.____

28

thing   that's   get-ting   in   the   way,___   when   we   go   up   to   bed_

___   you're   just   no   good,   it's   such   a   shame._____   I   look   in - to   your

eyes,   I   want   to   get   to   know___   you,   and   then   you   make   this

noise   and   it's   ap - par-ent   it's___   all   o - ver.

29

31

There's just one

thing   that's   get - ting   in   the   way,___   when   we   go   up   to   bed___   you're   just   no

good,   it's   such   a   shame.___   I   look   in - to   your   eyes,   I   want   to   get   to   know___

___   you,   and   then   you   make   this   noise   and   it's   ap - par - ent   it's___   all   o -

D.S. al Coda   ⊕ *Coda*

- ver.

33

OH MY GOD

WORDS & MUSIC BY NICHOLAS HODGSON, RICHARD WILSON,
ANDREW WHITE, JAMES RIX & NICHOLAS BAINES

8vb throughout

Time   on your side that will nev - er   end. The most beau - ti - ful thing you can ev - er   spend. But you

work   in a shirt with your name   tag   on it.   Drift - ing a - part like a plate   tec - ton - ic.

37

oh__ my god I__ can't be-lieve_ it. I've nev-er been this far a-way from__ home. An

oh__ my god I can't be-lieve_ it. I've nev-er been this far a-way from home._ An

oh__ my god I__ can't be-lieve_ it. I've nev-er been this far a-way from__ home._

1.

N.C.

And oh_ my god I_ can't be-lieve_ it. I've

nev-er been this far a-way from_ home. And oh_ my god I_ can't be-lieve_ it. I've

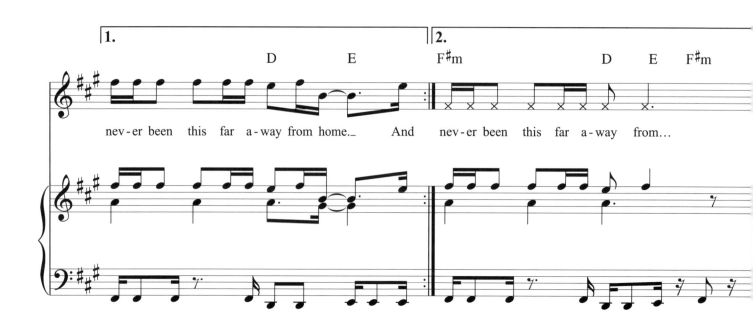

nev-er been this far a-way from home._ And nev-er been this far a-way from...

SMILE

WORDS & MUSIC BY LILY ALLEN, IYIOLA BABALOLA,
DARREN LEWIS & JACKIE MITTOO

1. When you first left me,___ I was want-ing more,___ but you were f**k-ing that girl next door; what'd you do that for?

(2.) -ev - er you see me,___ you say that you want me back, and I tell you it don't mean jack; no, it don't mean jack.

47

PART THREE

MADONNA

BORDERLINE

Somethin' in the way you love me
Won't let me be
I don't want to be your prisoner
So baby, won't you set me free

Stop playin' with my heart
Finish what you start
When you make my love come down
If you want me let me know
Baby, let it show
Honey, don't you fool around

Just try to understand
I've given all I can
'Cause you got the best of me

Borderline
Feels like I'm goin' to lose my mind
You just keep on pushin' my love
Over the borderline
Borderline
Feels like I'm goin' to lose my mind
You just keep on pushin' my love
Over the borderline

Somethin' in your eyes is makin'
Such a fool of me
When you hold me in your arms
You love me till I just can't see

But then you let me down
When I look around
Baby, you just can't be found
Stop drivin' me away
I just wanna stay
There's somethin' I just got to say

Just try to understand
I've given all I can
'Cause you got the best of me

Borderline
Feels like I'm goin' to lose my mind
You just keep on pushin' my love
Over the borderline
Borderline
Feels like I'm goin' to lose my mind
You just keep on pushin' my love
Over the borderline

Keep pushin' me
Keep pushin' me
Keep pushin' my love
Keep on pushin' my love
Over the borderline

Da da da da
Da da da da
Da da da da
You just keep on pushin' my love
Over the borderline

HOLIDAY

(Holiday, celebrate, holiday, celebrate)

If we took a holiday
Took some time to celebrate
Just one day out of life
It would be, it would be so nice

Everybody spread the word
We're gonna have a celebration
All across the world
In every nation

It's time for the good times
Forget about the bad times, oh yeah
One day, to come together
To release the pressure
We need a holiday

If we took a holiday
Took some time to celebrate
Just one day out of life
It would be, it would be so nice

You can turn this world around
And bring back all of those happy days
Put your troubles down
It's time to celebrate

Let love shine
And we will find
A way to come together
Can make things better
We need a holiday

If we took a holiday, (holiday)
Took some time to celebrate, (celebrate)
Just one day out of life, (just one day)
It would be, it would be so nice

(Holiday, celebrate, holiday, celebrate)

If we took a holiday, (Oh yeah, oh yeah)
Took some time to celebrate, (Come on, let's celebrate)
Just one day out of life, (holiday)
It would be, it would be so nice

(Holiday, celebrate, holiday)

HUNG UP

Time goes by so slowly
Time goes by so slowly
Time goes by so slowly
Time goes by so slowly
Time goes by so slowly
Time goes by so slowly

Every little thing that you say or do
I'm hung up
I'm hung up on you
Waiting for your call
Baby, night and day
I'm fed up
I'm tired of waiting on you

Time goes by so slowly for those who wait
No time to hesitate
Those who run seem to have all the fun
I'm caught up
I don't know what to do

Time goes by so slowly
Time goes by so slowly
Time goes by so slowly
I don't know what to do

Every little thing that you say or do
I'm hung up
I'm hung up on you
Waiting for your call
Baby, night and day
I'm fed up
I'm tired of waiting on you

Every little thing that you say or do
I'm hung up
I'm hung up on you
Waiting for your call
Baby, night and day
I'm fed up
I'm tired of waiting on you

Ring, ring, ring goes the telephone
The lights are on but there's no one home
Tick, tick, tock it's a quarter to two
And I'm done
I'm hanging up on you

I can't keep on waiting for you
I know that you're still hesitating
Don't cry for me
'Cause I'll find my way
You'll wake up one day
But it'll be too late

Every little thing that you say or do
I'm hung up
I'm hung up on you
Waiting for your call
Baby, night and day
I'm fed up
I'm tired of waiting on you

Every little thing that you say or do
I'm hung up
I'm hung up on you
Waiting for your call
Baby, night and day
I'm fed up
I'm tired of waiting on you

LIKE A VIRGIN

I made it through the wilderness
Somehow I made it through
Didn't know how lost I was
Until I found you

I was beat, incomplete
I'd been had, I was sad and blue
But you made me feel
Yeah, you made me feel shiny and new

Like a virgin
Touched for the very first time
Like a virgin
When your heart beats next to mine

Gonna give you all my love, boy
My fear is fadin' fast
Been savin' it all for you
'Cause only love can last

You're so fine, and you're mine
Make me strong, yeah, you make me bold
Oh, your love thawed out
Yeah, your love thawed out
What was scared and cold

Like a virgin, (hey)
Touched for the very first time
Like a virgin
With your heartbeat next to mine

Oh, oh, oh

You're so fine, and you're mine
I'll be yours till the end of time
'Cause you made me feel
Yeah, you made me feel
I've nothin' to hide

Like a virgin, (hey)
Touched for the very first time
Like a virgin
With your heartbeat next to mine

Like a virgin
Ooh, ooh, like a virgin
Feels so good inside
When you hold me
And your heart beats
And you love me

Like a virgin, ooh, ooh
Like a virgin
Feels so good inside
When you hold me
And your heart beats
And you love me

RAY OF LIGHT

Zephyr in the sky at night I wonder
Do my tears of mourning
Sink beneath the sun?

She's got herself a universe gone quickly
For the call of thunder
Threatens everyone

And I feel like I just got home, and I feel
And I feel like I just got home, and I feel

Faster than the speeding light she's flying
Trying to remember
Where it all began

She's got herself a little piece of heaven
Waiting for the time when
Earth shall be as one

And I feel like I just got home, and I feel
And I feel like I just got home, and I feel

Quicker than a ray of light
Quicker than a ray of light
Quicker than a ray of light

Zephyr in the sky at night I wonder
Do my tears of mourning
Sink beneath the sun?

She's got herself a universe gone quickly
For the call of thunder
Threatens everyone

And I feel
Quicker than a ray of light, then gone for
Someone else will be there
Through the endless years

She's got herself a universe
She's got herself a universe
She's got herself a universe

Said I feel, and I feel
And I feel like I just got home
And I feel

Quicker than a ray of light she's flying
Quicker than a ray of light I'm flying

YOU MUST LOVE ME

Where do we go from here?
This isn't where we intended to be
We had it all, you believed in me
I believed in you

Certainties disappear
What do we do for our dream to survive?
How do we keep all our passions alive
As we used to do?

Deep in my heart I'm concealing
Things that I'm longing to say
Scared to confess what I'm feeling
Frightened you'll slip away
You must love me
You must love me

Why are you at my side?
How can I be any use to you now?
Give me a chance, and I'll let you see how
Nothing has changed

Deep in my heart I'm concealing
Things that I'm longing to say
Scared to confess what I'm feeling
Frightened you'll slip away
You must love me
You must love me
You must love me

BORDERLINE

WORDS & MUSIC BY REGGIE LUCAS

Medium tempo

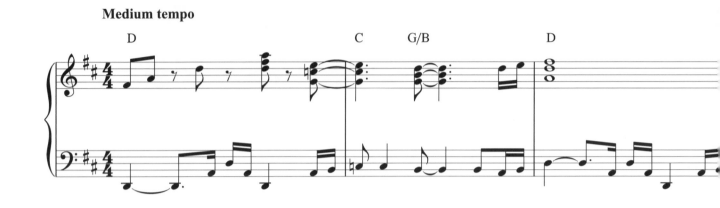

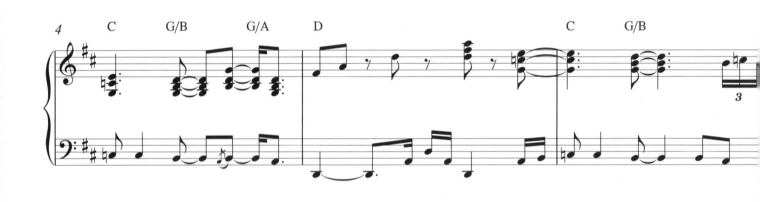

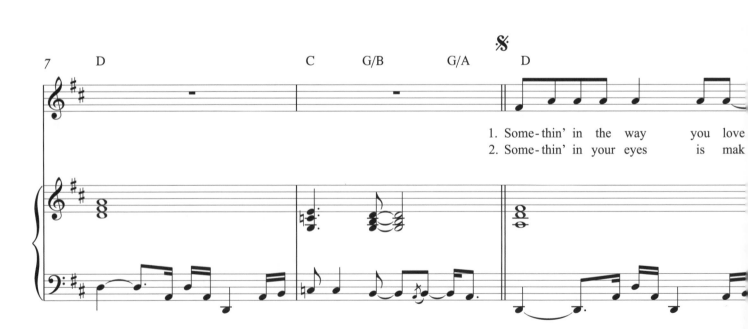

1. Some-thin' in the way   you love
2. Some-thin' in your eyes   is mak

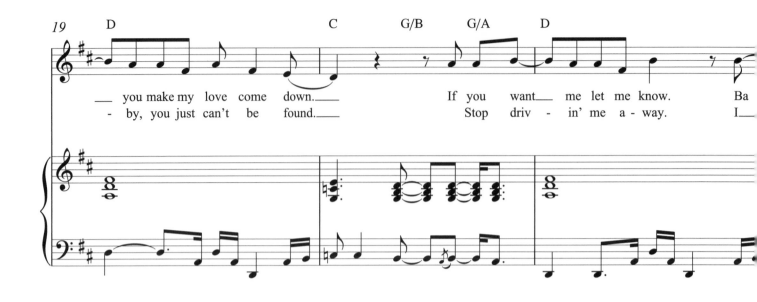

you make my love come down.___ If you want___ me let me know. Ba
- by, you just can't be found.___ Stop driv - in' me a - way. I

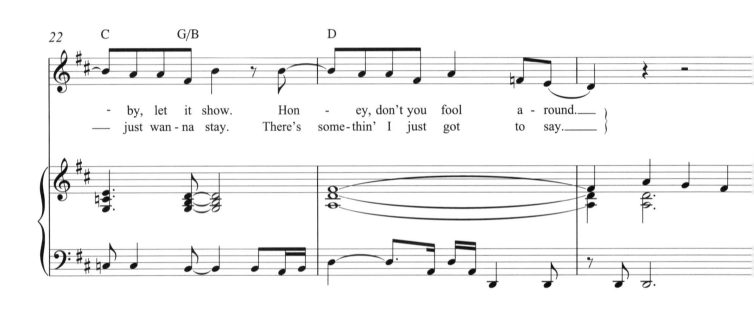

- by, let it show. Hon - ey, don't you fool a - round.___
___ just wan - na stay. There's some-thin' I just got to say.___

Just try___ to un - der - stand,___ I've giv

love   o - ver the bor - der - line.

13

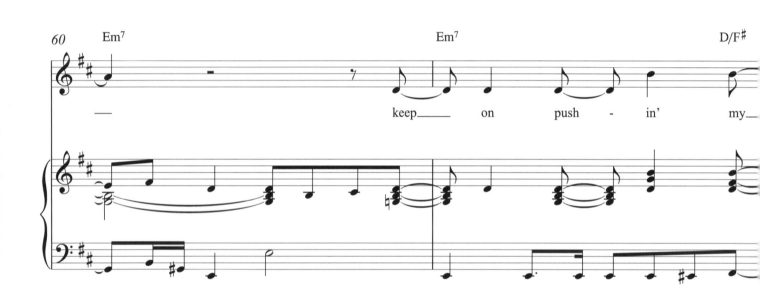

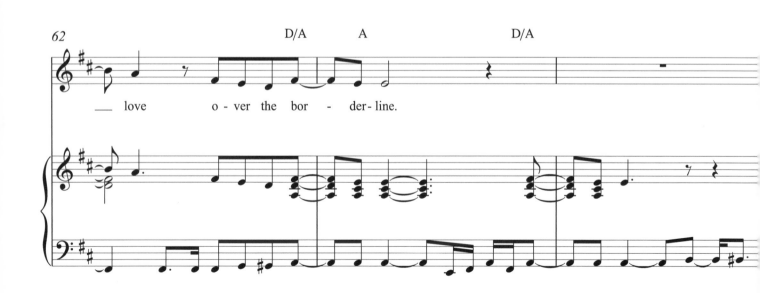

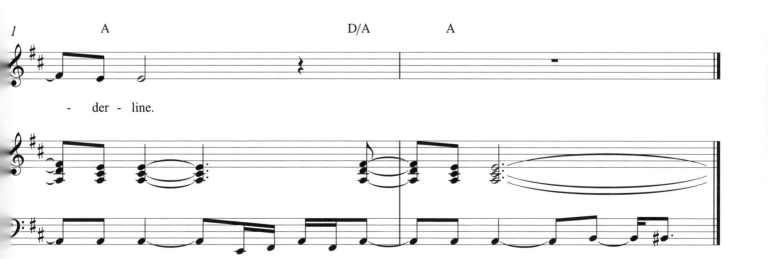

HOLIDAY

WORDS & MUSIC BY CURTIS HUDSON & LISA STEVENS

If we took a hol - i - day,___ took some time to cel - e - brate,___ just one day out of life,___ it would be,___ it would be so nice. Ev -'ry - bod - y spread_ the word:___ We're gon - na have a cel - e - bra -

HUNG UP

WORDS & MUSIC BY BENNY ANDERSSON, BJORN ULVAEUS,
MADONNA & STUART PRICE

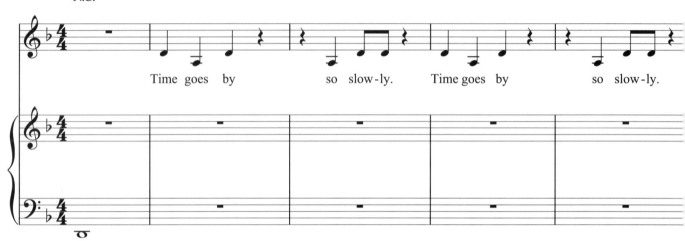

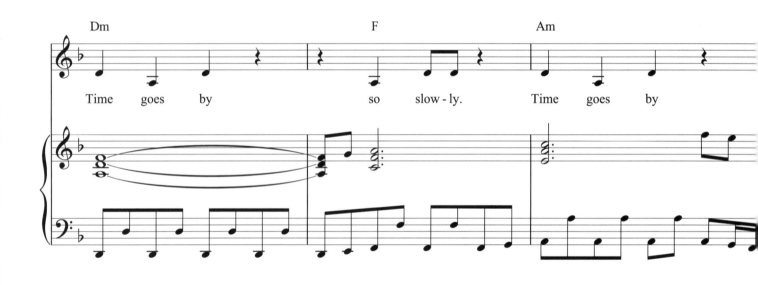

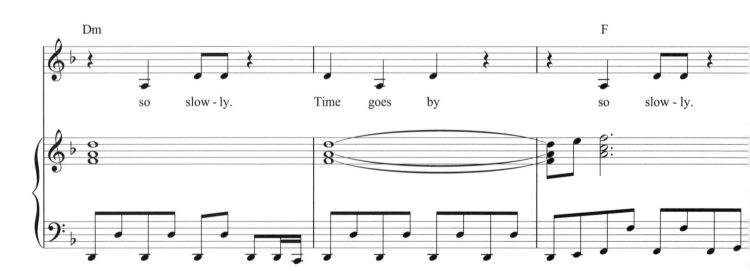

Time goes by so slow-ly.

Ev-'ry lit-tle thing that you say or do,___ I'm hung up;

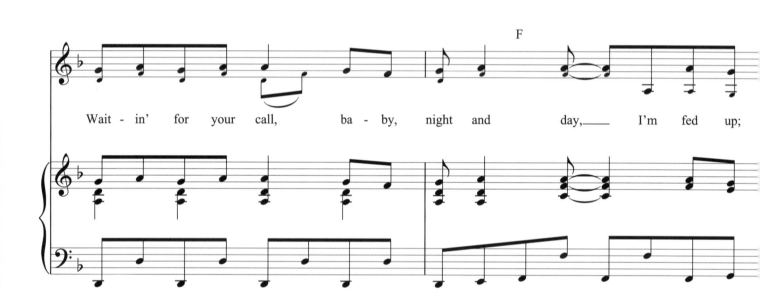

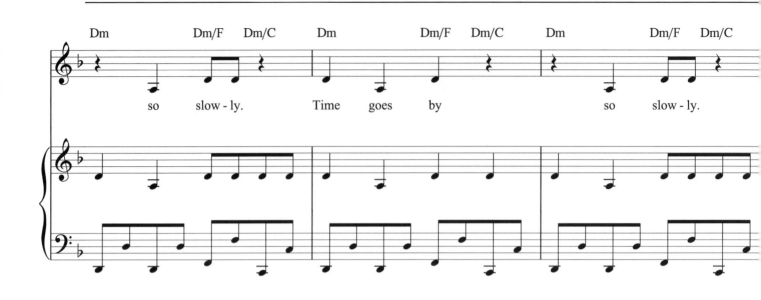

so slow - ly. Time goes by so slow - ly.

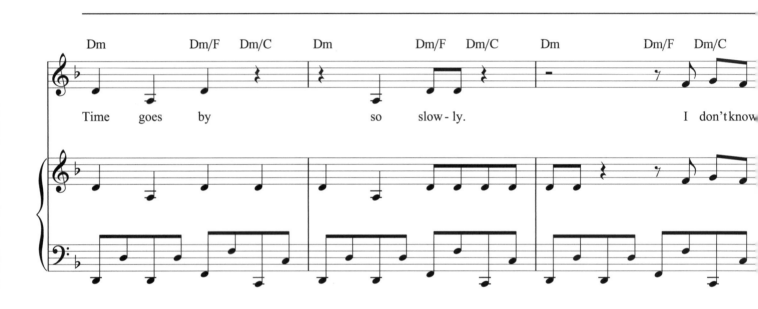

Time goes by so slow - ly. I don't know

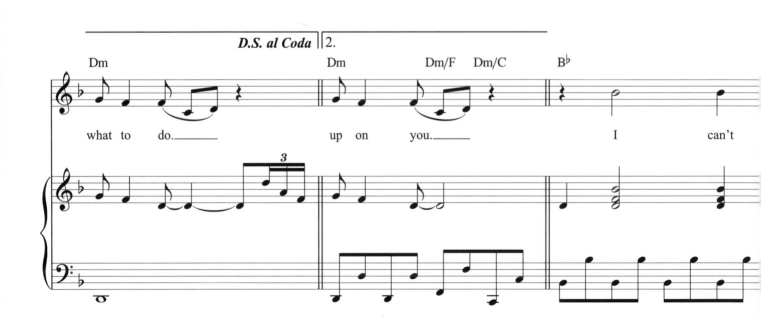

what to do._____ up on you._____ I can't

keep_____ on wait - ing_____ for you._____

I know that you're still___ hes - i - tat - ing.___

Don't cry for___ me, 'cause I'll find___

my way._____ You'll wake up_____ one_

day,_____ but it -'ll be too late._____ *(1st time only)*
Ev -'ry lit - tle thing that you

say or do,___ I'm hung up; I'm hung___ up on you._____

Wait-ing for your call, ba - by, night and day,___ I'm fed up; I'm tired of

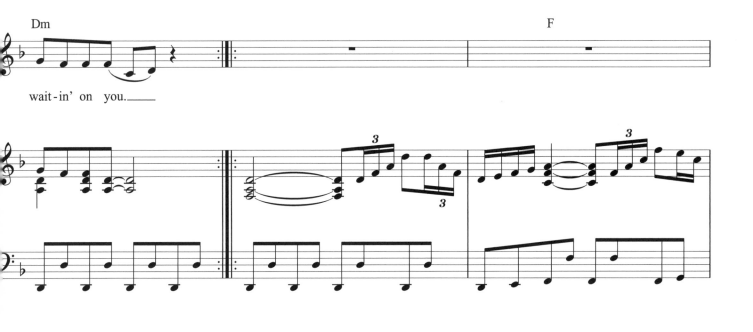

wait-in' on you.___

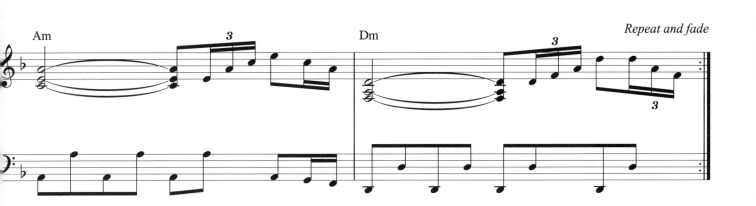

Repeat and fade

33

LIKE A VIRGIN

WORDS & MUSIC BY BILLY STEINBERG
& TOM KELLY

found you. ____ I was beat, ___ in-com-ple
love can last.___ You're so fine, ___ and you're mi
___ and you're mi

___ I'd been had.___ I was sad___ and blue.__ But you
___ Make me strong.___ Yeah, you make ___ me bold._ Oh, you
___ I'll be yours___ till the end___ of time._ 'Cause you

made me feel, ___ yeah, you made___ me fee
love thawed out, ___ yeah, your love___ thawed out
made me feel, ___ yeah, you made___ me feel

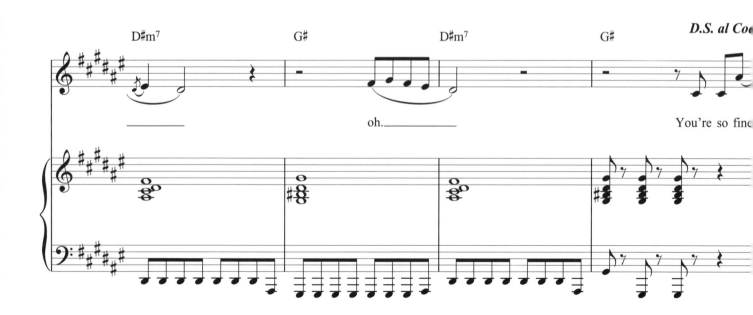

RAY OF LIGHT

WORDS & MUSIC BY MADONNA CICCONE, WILLIAM ORBIT, CLIVE MALDOON, DAVE CURTISS & CHRISTINE LEACH

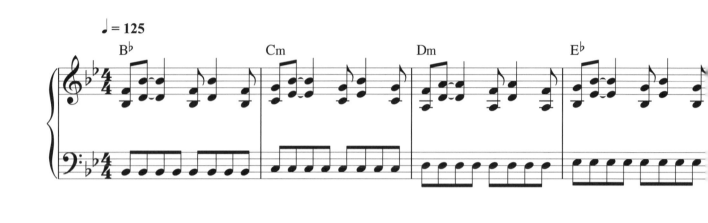

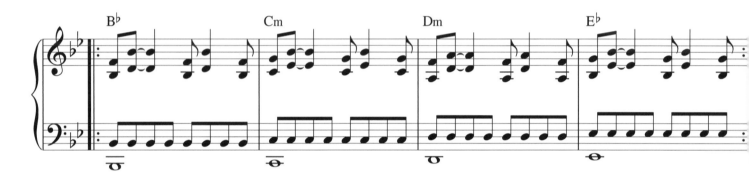

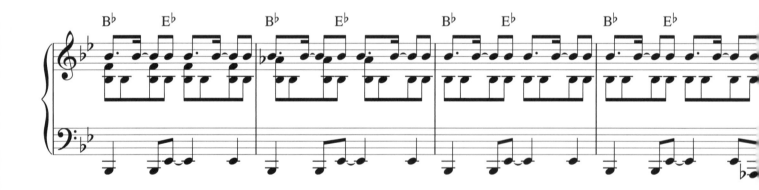

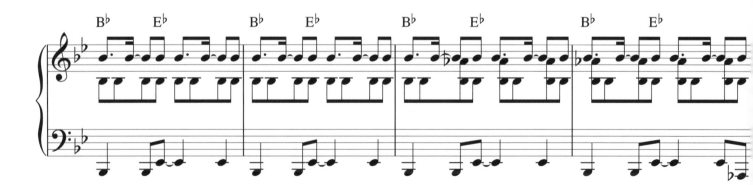

thun - der___ threat-ens ev - 'ry-one.
time when___ Earth shall be___ as one.

And I feel___ like I just___ got home.__ And I feel,

and I feel___ like I just___

___ got home.__ And I feel....

Ze-phyr in the sky___ at___ night_ I won - der:___ do my tears_ of___

...quick-er than a ray.

of light. Then gone for some-one else will

be there through the end - less years.

50

Quick-er than a ray____ of light__ she's fly - ing.__

Quick-er than a ray____ of light__ I'm____

fly - ing.__

Repeat to fade

51

YOU MUST LOVE ME

WORDS BY TIM RICE
MUSIC BY ANDREW LLOYD WEBBER

Tempo rubato ♩ = 100

Where do we go___ from here? This is-n't where we in-ten-ded to be.

We had it all,___ you be - lieved in me,___ I be - lieved in you.___

Cer-tain-ties dis-ap-pear.___ What do we do___ for our dream to sur-vive?

How do we keep all our pas-sions a - live,____ as we used to do?____

Deep in my heart____ I'm con-ceal - ing things that I'm long-ing to say.

Scared to con - fess____ what I'm feel - ing, fright-ened you'll slip____ a - way. You must love

me.

You must love me.

53

PART FOUR
WHITNEY HOUSTON

I HAVE NOTHING

Share my life, take me for what I am
'Cause I'll never change all my colours for you
Take my love, I'll never ask for too much
Just all that you are and everything that you do

I don't really need to look very much further
don't wanna have to go where you don't follow
I won't hold it back again, this passion inside
Can't run for myself, there's nowhere to hide

Oh, don't make me close one more door
I don't wanna hurt anymore
Stay in my arms if you dare
Or must I imagine you there
Don't walk away from me
I have nothing, nothing, nothing
If I don't have you, you, you, you, you

You see through right to the heart of me
break down my walls with the strength of your love
I never knew love like I've known it with you
Will a memory survive, one I can hold on to

I don't really need to look very much further
don't wanna have to go where you don't follow
I won't hold it back again, this passion inside
Can't run for myself, there's nowhere to hide
Your love I'll remember forever

Chorus

Don't make me close one more door
I don't wanna hurt anymore
Stay in my arms if you dare
Or must I imagine you there
Don't walk away from me
Don't walk away from me

Don't you dare walk away from me
I have nothing, nothing, nothing
if I don't have you, you
If I don't have you

I WANNA DANCE WITH SOMEBODY

The clock strikes upon the hour
And the sun begins to fade
There's still enough time to figure out
How to chase my blues away
I've done alright up till now
It's the light of day that shows me how
And when the night falls, loneliness calls

Oh, I wanna dance with somebody
I wanna feel the heat with somebody
Yeah, I wanna dance with somebody
With somebody who loves me
Oh, I wanna dance with somebody
I wanna feel the heat with somebody
Yeah, I wanna dance with somebody
With somebody who loves me

I've been in love and lost my senses
Spinning through the town
Sooner or later the feeling ends
And I wind up feeling down
I need a man who'll take a chance
On a love that burns hot enough to last
So when the night falls
My lonely heart calls

Chorus

Somebody who, somebody who
Somebody who loves me
Somebody who, somebody who
to hold me in his arms, oh

I need a man who'll take a chance
On a love that burns hot enough to last
So when the night falls, my lonely heart calls

Chorus

Repeat ad lib. to fade

I WILL ALWAYS LOVE YOU

If I should stay
I would only be in your way
So I'll go, but I know
I'll think of you every step of the way

And I will always love you
I will always love you
You, my darling you, mm

Bittersweet memories
That is all I'm taking with me
So goodbye, please don't cry
We both know I'm not what you, you need

And I will always love you
I will always love you

I hope life treats you kind
And I hope you have all you dreamed of
And I wish you joy and happiness
But above all this, I wish you love

And I will always love you
I will always love you
I will always love you
I, I will always love you
I will always love you
I, I will always love you
You, darling I love you

Ooh, I'll always, I'll always love you

DIDN'T WE ALMOST HAVE IT ALL

Remember when we held on in the rain
The nights we almost lost it once again
We can take the night into tomorrow
Living on feelings
Touching you I feel it all again

Didn't we almost have it all
when love was all we had worth giving
The ride with you was worth the fall
My friend

Loving you makes life worth living
Didn't we almost have it all
The nights we held on till the morning
You'll know you'll never love that way again
Didn't we almost have it all

The way you used to touch me felt so fine
We kept our hearts together down the line
A moment in the soul can last forever
Comfort and keep us
Help me bring the feelings back again

Chorus

e have the best of times when love was young and new
dn't we reach inside and find a world of me and you
We'll never lose it again
'Cos once you know what love is
You never let it end

Didn't we almost have it all
The nights we held on till the morning
You know you'll never love that way again
Didn't we almost have it all
Didn't we almost have it all

RUN TO YOU

I know that when you look at me
There's so much that you just don't see
But if you would only take the time
I know in my heart you'd find
Oh, a girl who's scared sometimes
Who isn't always strong
Can't you see the hurt in me
I feel so all alone

I wanna run to you, hoo, hoo
I wanna run to you, hoo, hoo, hoo
Won't you hold me in your arms
And keep me safe from harm
I wanna run to you, hoo, hoo
But if I come to you, hoo, hoo, hoo
Tell me, will you stay or will you run away

Each day, each day I play the role
Of someone always in control
But at night I come home and turn the key
There's nobody there, no one cares for me
Oh, what's the sense of trying hard to find your dreams
Without someone to share them with
Tell me, what does it mean

Chorus
Run away

I need you here
I need you here to wipe away my tears
To kiss away my fears
If you only knew how much

I want to run to you, hoo, hoo
I wanna run to you, hoo, hoo, hoo
Won't you hold me in your arms
And keep me safe from harm
I wanna run to you, hoo, hoo
But if I come to you, hoo, hoo, hoo
Tell me, will you stay or will you run away

SAVING ALL MY LOVE FOR YOU

A few stolen moments is all that we share
You've got your family and they need you there
Though I try to resist, being last on your list
But no other man's gonna do
So I'm saving all my love for you

It's not very easy living all alone
My friends try and tell me find a man of my own
But each time I try, I just break down and cry
'Cause I'd rather be home feelin' blue
So I'm saving all my love for you

You used to tell me we'd run away together
Love gives you the right to be free
You said: "Be patient, just wait a little longer"
But that's just an old fantasy

I've got to get ready, just a few minutes more
Gonna get that old feeling when you walk through that door
'Cause tonight is the night for feeling alright
We'll be making love the whole night through
So I'm saving all my love
Yes I'm saving all my love
Yes I'm saving all my love for you

No other woman is gonna love you more
'Cause tonight is the night that I'm feeling alright
We'll be making love the whole night through
So I'm saving all my love
Yes I'm saving all my loving
Yes I'm saving all my love for you
For you

I HAVE NOTHING

WORDS & MUSIC BY DAVID FOSTER & LINDA THOMPSON JENNER

5

8

9

close _____ one more door, I don't wan - na hurt _____ a - ny - more. ___ Stay in my arms _____ if you dare ____ or must I i - - ma - gine you there? ____ Don't walk a - way from me. ____ Don't walk a - way from me. ____ Don't you dare walk a - way from me. _____ I have

I WANNA DANCE WITH SOMEBODY
(WHO LOVES ME)

WORDS & MUSIC BY GEORGE MERRILL & SHANNON RUBICAM

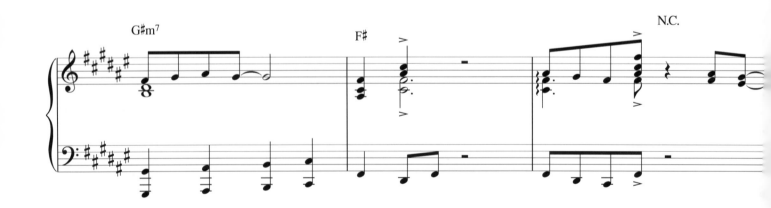

1. The clock strikes up - on the hour and the sun be - gins to fade.
(Verse 2 see block lyric)

There's still e - nough time to fig - ure out how to chase my blues a - way.

I've done al - right up till now, it's the light of day that shows

___ me how___ and when the night_ falls,___ lone - li - ness calls._

_Oh,___ I wan - na dance___ with some - bod - y, I wan - na feel the hea_

___ with some - bod - y, yeah,___ I wan - na dance___ with some - bod - y,_

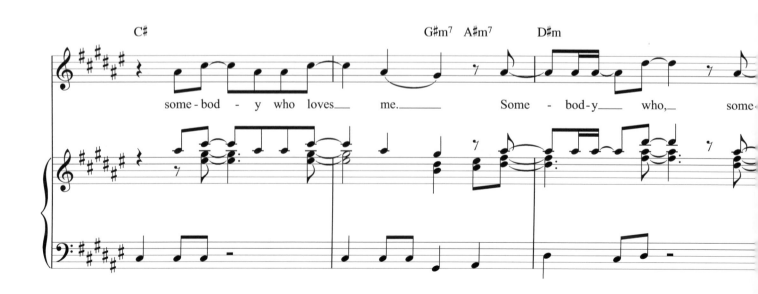

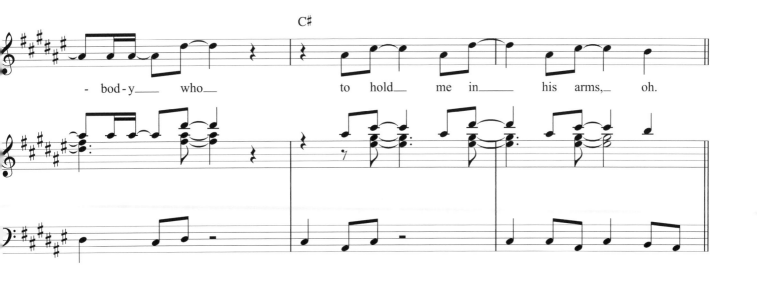

-bod-y___ who___ to hold___ me in___ his arms,___ oh.

I need a man who'll take___ a chance___ on a love___ that burns___ hot e-nough___

___ to last,___ so when the night___ falls,___ my lone-ly heart calls.

Verse 2

I've been in love and lost my senses
Spinning through the town
Sooner or later the feeling ends
And I wind up feeling down
I need a man who'll take a chance
On a love that burns hot enough to last
So when the night falls
My lonely heart calls

I WILL ALWAYS LOVE YOU

WORDS & MUSIC BY DOLLY PARTON

think of you____ ev - 'ry step____ of the way.____

a tempo (♩ = 60)

And I____ will al - ways

love you,____ I____ will____ al - ways

poco accel.

love you,____ you,____ my

21

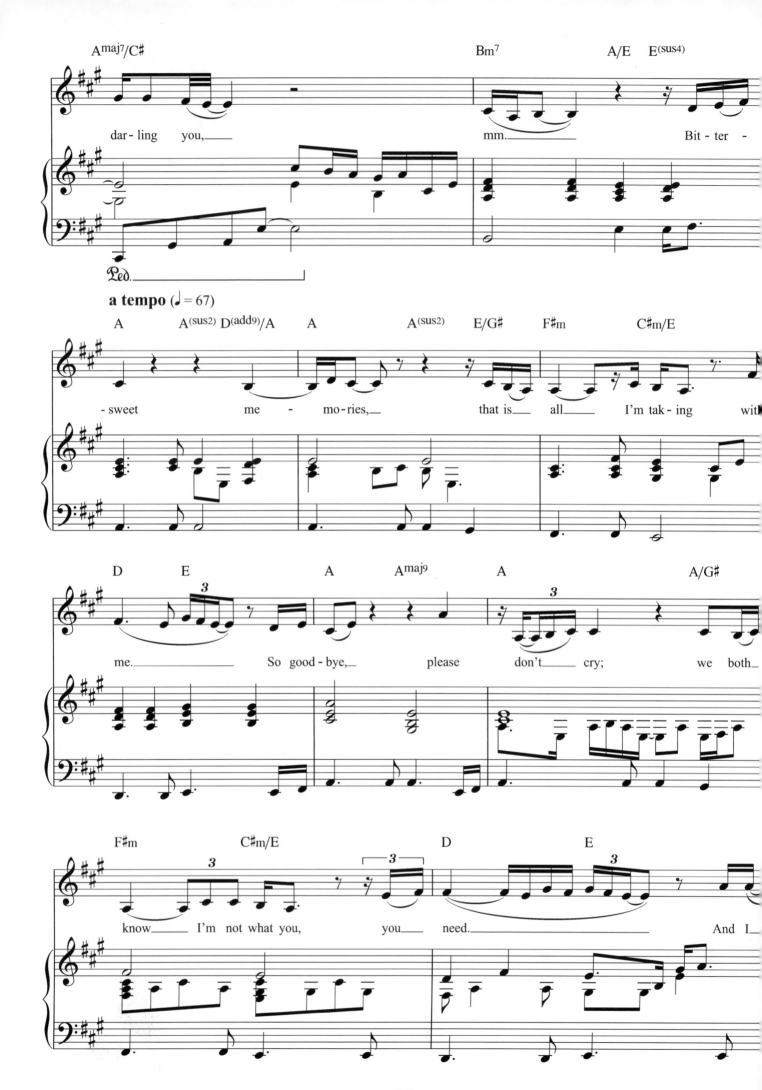

22

will al - ways love you,_____ I

will al - ways love_ you._____

(1st time saxophone solo)
(2.) hope   life__ treats you___ kind,___   and I___ hope_____ you have all you   dreamed

of._____   And I wish you joy   and___ hap - pi - ness:_____   but, a - bove all___

24

I will al - ways lo - ve you,

rit.

I, I will al - ways love you

a tempo

you, you. Dar - ling I

molto rit.

love you. Ooh, I'll al - ways, I'll al - ways love you.

25

DIDN'T WE ALMOST HAVE IT ALL

WORDS & MUSIC BY WILL JENNINGS & MICHAEL MASSER

we can take the night__ in - to to - mor - row_____ liv-ing on

feel - ings,_____ touch-ing you__ I feel it all a - gain.__

Did-n't we al - most have it all,__ when love was all we had worth

giv-ing.___ The ride with you was worth the fall my friend,_

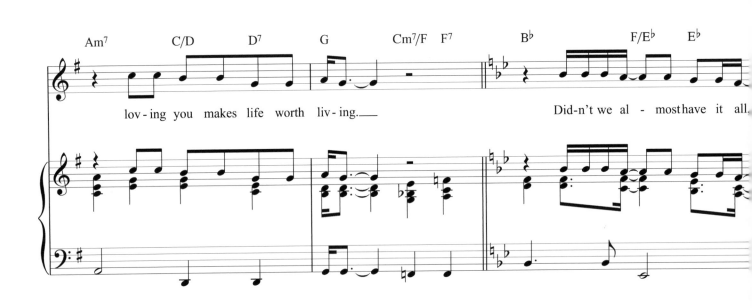

lov-ing you makes life worth liv-ing.___ Did-n't we al - most have it all,

the nights we held on till the morn - ing.___

could-n't we reach in - side_ and find_ a world of me and you,_ we'll nev - er

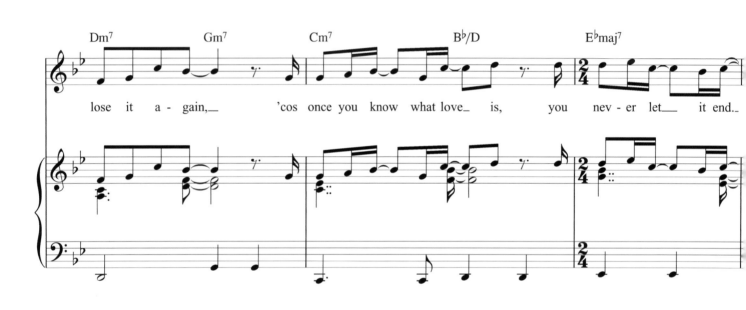

lose it a - gain,_ 'cos once you know what love_ is, you nev - er let_ it end._

Did-n't we al - most have it all___

Verse 2

The way you used to touch me felt so fine
We kept our hearts together down the line
A moment in the soul can last forever
Comfort and keep us
Help me bring the feelings back again

33

RUN TO YOU

WORDS & MUSIC BY JUD FRIEDMAN & ALLAN RICH

37

40

SAVING ALL MY LOVE FOR YOU

WORDS & MUSIC BY GERRY GOFFIN & MICHAEL MASSER

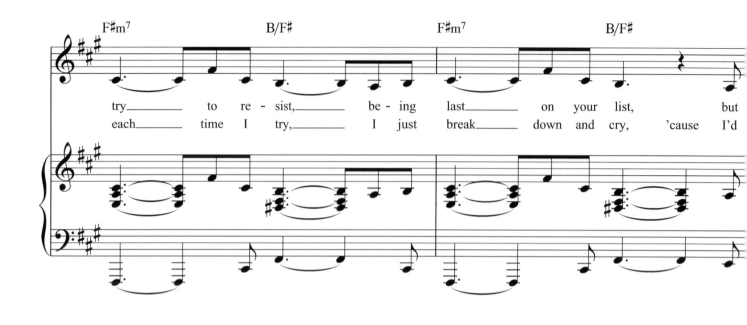

try_____ to re - sist,_____ be - ing last_____ on your list, but
each_____ time I try,_____ I just break_____ down and cry, 'cause I'd

no oth - er man's_____ gon - na do._____
rath - er be home_____ feel - in' blue._____ So I'm

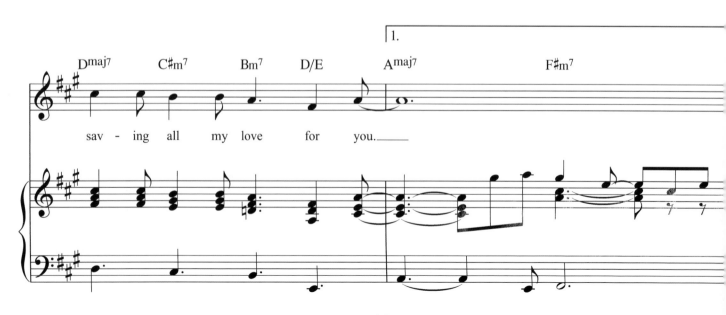

sav - ing all my love for you._____

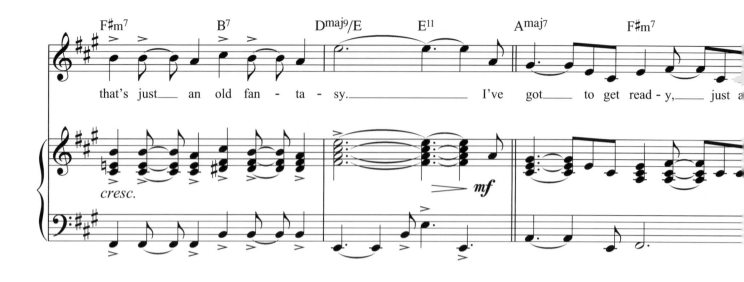

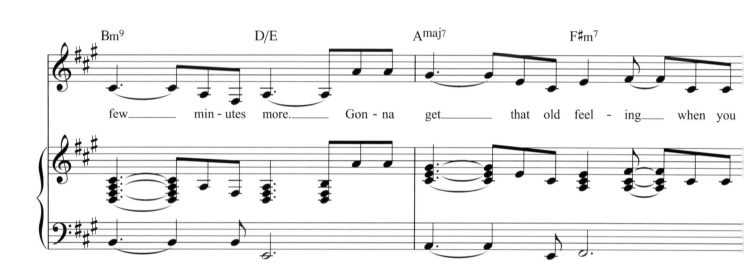

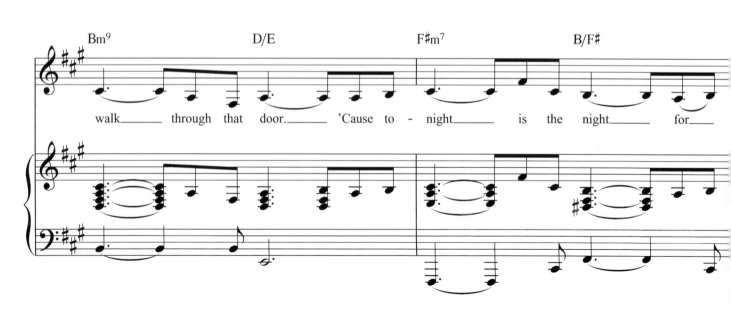

feel - ing al - right._____ We'll be mak - ing love the whole night____

through,_____ so I'm sav - ing all my love, yes I'm sav - ing all my love, yes I'm

sav - ing all my love for___ you._____

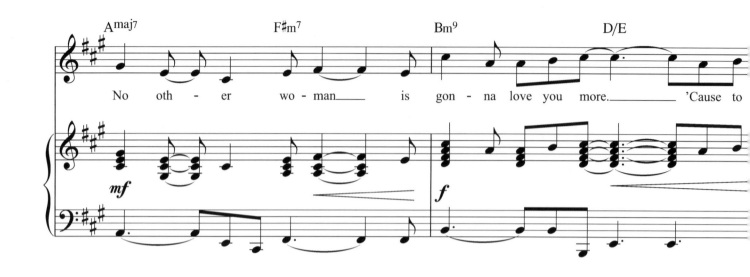

No oth - er wo - man___ is gon - na love you more.___ 'Cause to

- night___ is the night___ that I'm feel - ing al - right.___ We'll be

mak - ing love the whole___ night___ through;___ so I'm

47

PART FIVE
MARIAH CAREY

AGAINST ALL ODDS
(TAKE A LOOK AT ME NOW)

How can I just let you walk away
Just let you leave without a trace
When I stand here taking every breath
With you, ooh
You're the only one
Who really knew me at all

How can you just walk away from me
When all I can do is watch you leave
'Cause we've shared the laughter and the pain
And even shared the tears
You're the only one
Who really knew me at all

So take a look at me now
'Cause there's just an empty space
There's nothing left here to re-mind me
Just the memory of your face
Oh, take a look at me now
Well, there's just an empty space
And you comin' back to me
Is against the odds
And that's what I've got to face

I wish I could just make you turn around
Turn around and see me cry
There's so much I need to say to you
So many reasons why
You're the only one
Who really knew me at all

So take a look at me now
Well, there's just an empty space
There's nothing left here to remind me
Just the memory of you face
Oh, take a look at me now
So there's just an empty space
But to wait for you
Is all I can do
And that's what I've got to face

Take a good look at me now
'Cause I'll still be standing here
And you com-in' back to me
Is against all odds
That's the chance I've got to take, yeah

Take a look at me now
Take a look at me now
Take a look at me now

ALL I WANT FOR CHRISTMAS IS YOU

I don't want a lot for Christmas
There is just one thing I need
I don't care about the presents
Underneath the Christmas tree
I just want you for my own
More than you could ever know
Make my wish come true
All I want for Christmas is you, yeah

I don't want a lot for Christmas
There is just one thing I need
(And I...) Don't care about the presents
Underneath the Christmas tree
I don't need to hang my stocking
There upon the fireplace
Santa Claus won't make me happy
With a toy on Christmas day
I just want you for my own
More than you could ever know
Make my wish come true
All I want for Christmas is you, you, baby

Oh, I won't ask for much this Christmas
I won't even wish for snow
(And I...) I'm just gonna keep on waiting
Underneath the mistletoe
I won't make a list and send it
To the North Pole for Saint Nick
I won't even stay awake to
Hear those magic reindeer click
I just want you here tonight
Holding on to me so tight
What more can I do
Baby, all I want for Christmas is you, you, baby

Oh, All the lights are shining
So brightly everywhere
And the sound of children's
Laughter fills the air
And everyone is singing
I hear those sleigh bells ringing
Santa won't you please
Bring me what I really need
Won't you please bring my baby to me

Oh, I don't want a lot for Christmas
This is all I'm asking for
I just want to see my baby
Standing right outside my door
I just want him for my own
More than you could ever know
Make my wish come true
All I want for Christmas is you, ooh, baby
All I want for Christmas is you, baby
All I want for Christmas is you, baby

Repeat to fade

HERO

There's a hero
If you look inside your heart
You don't have to be afraid
Of what you are
There's an answer
If you reach into your soul
And the sorrow that you know
Will melt away

And then a hero comes along
With the strength to carry on
And you cast your fears aside
And you know you can survive
So, when you feel like hope is gone
look inside you and be strong
And you'll finally see the truth
That a hero lies in you

It's a long road
When you face the world alone
No one reaches out a hand
For you to hold
You can find love
If you search within yourself
And the emptiness you felt
Will disappear

And then a hero comes along
With the strength to carry on
And you cast your fears aside
And you know you can survive
So, when you feel like hope is gone
look inside you and be strong
And you'll finally see the truth
That a hero lies in you

Lord knows
Dreams are hard to follow
But don't let anyone
Tear them away
Hold
There will be tomorrow
In time you'll find the way

And then a hero comes along
With the strength to carry on
And you cast your fears aside
And you know you can survive
So, when you feel like hope is gone
look inside you and be strong
And you'll finally see the truth
That a hero lies in you

That a hero lies in you
That a hero lies in you

MY ALL

Nah, nah, mm
I am thinking of you
In my sleepless solitude tonight
If it's wrong to love you
Then my heart just won't let me be right
'Cause I'm drowned in you
And I won't move through
Without you by my side

I'd give my all to have
Just one more night with you
I'd risk my life to feel
Your body next to mine
'Cause I can't go on
Living in the memory of our song
I'd give my all
For your love tonight

Baby can you feel me
Imagining I'm looking in your eyes
I can see you clearly
Vividly emblazoned in my mind
And yet you're so far
Like a distant star
I'm wishing on tonight

I'd give my all to have
Just one more night with you
I'd risk my life to feel
Your body next to mine
'Cause I can't go on
Living in the memory of our song
I'd give my all
For your love tonight

Instrumental

I'd give my all to have
Just one more night with you
I'd risk my life to feel
Your body next to mine
'Cause I can't go on
Living in the memory of our song
I'd give my all
For your love tonight
Give my all
For your love tonight

WE BELONG TOGETHER

Ooh, oh, ooh, oh, sweet love
I didn't mean it when I said I didn't love you so
I should've held on tight I never should've let you go
I didn't know nothing I was stupid I was foolish
I was lying to myself

I could not fathom I would ever be without your love
Never imagine I'd be sitting here beside myself
'Cause didn't know you, 'cause I didn't know me
But I thought I knew everything I never felt

The feeling that I'm feeling now that I don't hear your voice
Or have your touch and kiss your lips 'cause I don't have a choice
Oh, what I wouldn't give to have you lying by my side
Right here, 'cause baby

When you left I lost a part of me
It's still so hard to believe
Come back, baby, please
'Cause we belong together

Who else am I gonna lean on when times get rough
Who's gonna talk to me on the phone till the sun comes up
Who's gonna take your place, there ain't nobody better
Oh, baby, baby we belong together

I can't sleep at night when you are on my mind
Bobby Womack's on the radio saying to me
"If you think you're lonely now"
Wait a minute this is too deep
(Too deep) I gotta change the station

So I turn the dial trying to catch a break
And then I hear Babyface
I only think of you and it's breaking my heart
I'm trying to keep it together but I'm falling apart

I'm feeling all out of my element throwing things, crying
Trying to figure out where the hell I went wrong
The pain reflected in this song ain't even half of what
I'm feeling inside I need you, need you back in my life, baby

When you left I lost a part of me
It's still so hard to believe
Come back, baby, please
'Cause we belong together

Who else am I gonna lean on when times get rough
Who's gonna talk to me on the phone till the sun comes up
Who's gonna take your place, there ain't nobody better
Oh, baby, baby we belong together

When you left I lost a part of me
It's still so hard to believe
Come back, baby, please
'Cause we belong together

Who am I gonna lean on when times get rough
Who's gonna talk to me till the sun comes up
Who's gonna take your place there ain't nobody better
Oh, baby, baby we belong together

Repeat ad lib. to fade

WHEN YOU BELIEVE

Many nights we pray
With no proof anyone could hear
In our hearts a hopeful song
We barely understand

Now we are not afraid
Although we know there's much to fear
We were moving mountains long
Before we knew we could

There can be miracles
When you believe
Though hope is frail
It's hard to kill

Who knows what miracles
You can achieve
When you believe
Somehow you will
You will when you believe, ooh

In this time of fear
When prayer so often proves in vain
Hope seems like the summer birds
Too swiftly flown away
Yet now I'm standing here
My heart's so full I can't explain
Seeking faith and speaking words
I never thought I'd say

There can be miracles
When you believe
Though hope is frail
It's hard to kill

Who knows what miracles
You can achieve
When you believe
Somehow you will
You will when you believe

They don't always happen when you ask
And it's easy to give in to your fears
But when you're blinded by your pain
Can't see your way straight through the rain
A small but still resilient voice says love is very near

There can be miracles
When you believe
Though hope is frail
It's hard to kill

Who knows what miracles
You can achieve
When you believe
Somehow you will

Now you will

Vocal ad lib.

You will when you believe
You will when you believe
You will when you believe

AGAINST ALL ODDS
(TAKE A LOOK AT ME NOW)

WORDS & MUSIC BY PHIL COLLINS

1. How can I just let you walk away, just let you leave without a trace, when I stand here taking ev'ry breath with you? Ooh, you're the

on - ly one who real - ly knew me at all.

2. How can you just walk a-way from me when all I can do is watch you leave? 'Cause we'
(Verse 3 see block lyric)

shared the laugh - ter and the pain, and ev - en shared the tears. You're th

on - ly one who real - ly knew me at all. So take a look at me now

10

11

Verse 3:

I wish I could just make you turn around
Turn around and see me cry
There's so much I need to say to you
So many reasons why
You're the only one
Who really knew me at all

So take a look at me now
Well, there's just an empty space
There's nothing left here to remind me
Just the memory of you face
Oh, take a look at me now
So there's just an empty space
But to wait for you is all I can do
And that's what I've got to face

13

ALL I WANT FOR CHRISTMAS IS YOU

WORDS & MUSIC BY MARIAH CAREY
& WALTER AFANASIEFF

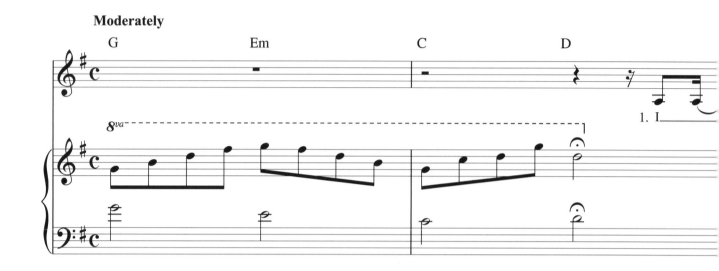

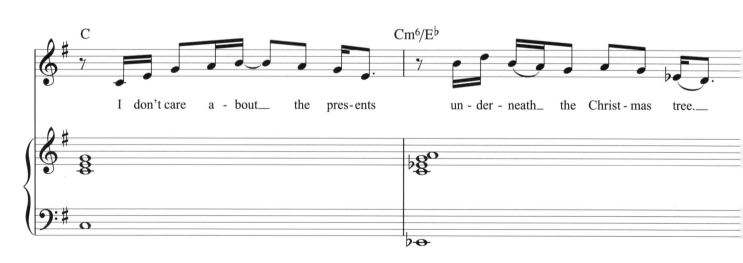

D. S. al Coda

19

20

HERO

WORDS & MUSIC BY MARIAH CAREY
& WALTER AFANASIEFF

Moderately

1. There's a he - ro if you look in - side your heart. You don't
2. long road when you face the world a - lone. No one

have to be a - fraid of what you are. There's an an -
reach - es out a hand for you to hold.

- swer if you reach in - to your soul and the
love if you search with - in your - self and the

sor - row that__ you know__ will melt a - way.__
emp - ti - ness__ you felt__ will dis - ap - pear.__

And then a he - ro comes__ a - long__ with the strength to car - ry on__

__ and you cast your fears__ a - side__ and you know you can__ sur - vive.__

__ So, when you feel like hope__ is gone__ look in - side you and__ be strong__

25

and you'll fin - 'ly see___ the truth___ that a he - ro lies___ in you.___

It's a ___

Lord knows_____ dreams are hard___ to fol - low,

but don't let an - y - one___ tear them a - way.___

26

MY ALL

WORDS BY MARIAH CAREY

MUSIC BY MARIAH CAREY & WALTER AFANASIEFF

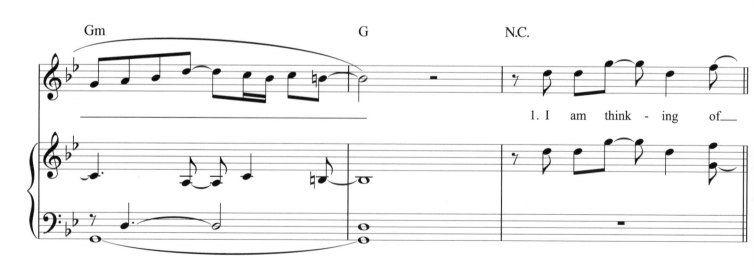

WE BELONG TOGETHER

WORDS & MUSIC BY MARIAH CAREY, JERMAINE DUPRI, KENNETH EDMONDS,
MANUEL SEAL, BOBBY WOMACK, DARNELL BRISTOL, SIDNEY JOHNSON,
JOHNTA AUSTIN, PATRICK MOTEN & SANDRA SULLY

34

WHEN YOU BELIEVE

WORDS & MUSIC BY STEPHEN SCHWARTZ

Man-y nights we pray with no proof a-ny-one could hear. In our hearts a hope-ful song we

bare-ly__ un-der-stand. Now we are not__ a-fraid__ al-though we know there's much to fear.

43

45

CD BACKING TRACKS

PART 1

1. **Chasing Pavements**
(Adkins/White) Universal Music Publishing Limited

2. **Hometown Glory**
(Adkins) Universal Music Publishing Limited

3. **Make You Feel My Love**
(Dylan) Sony/ATV Music Publishing (UK) Limited

4. **Rolling In The Deep**
(Adkins/Epworth) Universal Music Publishing Limited/EMI Music Publishing Limited

5. **Set Fire To The Rain**
(Smith/Adkins) Chrysalis Music Limited/Universal Music Publishing Limited

6. **Someone Like You**
(Adkins/Wilson) Universal Music Publishing Limited/Chrysalis Music Limited

PART 2

1. **22**
(Allen/Kurstin) Universal Music Publishing Limited/EMI Music Publishing Limited

2. **The Fear**
(Allen/Kurstin) Universal Music Publishing Limited/EMI Music Publishing Limited

3. **LDN**
(Babalola/Lewis/Allen/Reid) Universal Music Publishing Limited/Sparta Florida Music Group Limited

4. **Not Fair**
(Allen/Kurstin) Universal Music Publishing Limited/EMI Music Publishing Limited

5. **Oh My God**
(Hodgson/Wilson/White/Rix/Baines) Imagem Music Limited

6. **Smile**
(Allen/Babalola/Lewis/Mittoo) Universal Music Publishing Limited/
Sparta Florida Music Group Limited

PART 3

1. **Borderline**
(Lucas) Universal Music Publishing MGB Limited

2. **Holiday**
(Hudson/Stevens) Warner/Chappell Music Limited

3. **Hung Up**
(Andersson/Ulvaeus/Madonna/Price) Bocu Music Limited/Warner/Chappell Music Limited

4. **Like A Virgin**
(Steinberg/Kelly) Sony/ATV Music Publishing (UK) Limited

5. **Ray Of Light**
(Ciccone/Orbit/Maldoon/Curtiss/Leach)
Imagem Songs Limited/Warner/Chappell Music Limited/Purple Music Limited

6. **You Must Love Me**
(Webber/Rice) Evita Music Limited

PART 4

1. **I Have Nothing**
(Foster/Jenner) Warner/Chappell Music Limited/Peermusic (UK) Limited

2. **I Wanna Dance With Somebody (Who Loves Me)**
(Merrill/Rubicam) Universal Music Publishing Limited

3. **I Will Always Love You**
(Parton) Carlin Music Corporation

4. **Didn't We Almost Have It All**
(Jennings/Masser) Universal/MCA Music Limited

5. **Run To You**
(Friedman/Rich) Peermusic (UK) Limited/Universal/MCA Music Limited

6. **Saving All My Love For You**
(Goffin/Masser) EMI Music Publishing Limited/Universal/MCA Music Limited

PART 5

1. **Against All Odds (Take A Look At Me Now)**
(Collins) Imagem Music

2. **All I Want For Christmas Is You**
(Carey/Afanasieff) Sony/ATV Music Publishing (UK) Limited/Universal/MCA Music Limited

3. **Hero**
(Carey/Afanasieff) Universal/MCA Music Limited/Warner/Chappell North America Limited

4. **My All**
(Carey/Afanasieff) Sony/ATV Music Publishing (UK) Limited/Universal/MCA Music Limited

5. **We Belong Together**
(Carey/Dupri/Edmonds/Seal/Womack/Bristol/Johnson/Austin/Moten/Sully)
Universal Music Publishing MGB Limited/EMI Music Publishing Limited/Universal/MCA Music Limited/
ABKCO Music Limited/Chrysalis Music Limited/Sony/ATV Music Publishing (UK) Limited/
Sandra E Sully/Warner/Chappell North America/Copyright Control

6. **When You Believe**
(Schwartz) Cherry Lane Music Publishing Company Incorporated